Random Riffs

Poems by Ken Gierke

Spartan Press

Spartan Press

Kansas City, Missouri

Spartan Press

Copyright © Ken Gierke, 2025

First Edition: 1 3 5 7 9 10 8 6 4 2

ISBN: 979-8-89975-008-3

LCCN: 2025938309

Cover and title page images: Ken Gierke

Author photo: Bonnie Close

"In his latest collection, *Random Riffs* (Spartan Press), poet Ken Gierke invites the reader to 'take a drive' with him and Mingus, Coltrane or Monk, or to glide along with him and Nina Simone as he kayaks his favorite streams. Gierke's poems, written to the beats of his eclectic musical playlist take the reader on a journey, sometimes whimsically inspired by the Grateful Dead, sometimes tuned to the more solemn notes of Mingus or Mozart. In this new collection, the beat goes on, giving the reader a glimpse into his life, inspired by his personal musical favorites like The Who, Hendrix, Brubeck, the Beatles, Mingus, Monk, Mozart, or Coltrane. This collection is not really a 'long strange trip', but an inspired collection. Accessible, easy to read, each poem is alive with the beats of his playlist in each line."

-Sharon SingingMoon, author of *Random Seed* and
The Weight of One Hummingbird Feather

"I have just completed Ken Gierke's new Chapbook *Random Riffs* and I don't need any other reasons to love this collection other than the spare rhythmic cadence of his words and the road that has spawned them. But I also have the fact that so many of these poems draw added parental DNA from the songs that inspired them. Ken writes great poetry, but he also has amazing taste in music. From John Coltrane to George Thoroughgood, he finds the aesthetic center of each song and composer he listens to on his long road trips and communicates that ephemeral something found in all good music into words on the page. Most of these poems were written on the fly. He dictated them into his phone in real time while traveling throughout our country. I highly recommend this collection to anyone who loves words and who wants to get an even deeper understanding of how music shapes our perceptions as we travel on our chosen roads."

-Rick Christiansen, author of *Bone Fragments*
(Spartan Press 2024)

"I once was young, / and life was always long," Ken Gierke thinks to himself as he and the reader are transported along for the ride: the long road to wherever the hell we are now. Gierke's *Random Riffs* aren't random at all. These are the meaningful musings of the open-road samurai, armed with unleaded gasoline and a well-curated playlist of jazz and classic rock. Gierke's poems will make you want to put on your favorite songs and hit the open road; you may even be surprised where you'll want to drive. This isn't escapist freewheeling or some kind of neo-Kerouac treatise on road trips and their eventual brush with bop. This is classic Gierke: relatable, moving, expressive. These poems hit hard because Gierke knows that even the simplest moments and even the most familiar songs stand much bigger than their surface impressions. Whether it's some backwoods highway or a Coltrane classic, "we both know / there's got to be one helluva story behind it."

-Timothy Tarkelly, author of *A Horse Called Victory* and *The You We Know and Love.*

Acknowledgments

Special thanks go to the editors of the following publications where these poems first appeared:

Trailer Park Quarterly: "Driving with Brubeck,"

As It Ought to Be Magazine: "Riding with Monk," "After the Rain,"

Rusty Truck: "Ascenseur pour l'echafaud ," "Riding in Comfort to Kingston," and "Rainy Day,"

River Dog Zine: "Frank Morgan at the Wheel," "Leaving Wyoming with Mingus," "Drivin' Under the Influence," "Drivin' with Primus," and "A Love Supreme,"

The Rye Whiskey Review: "Leaving Kansas with Jimi," "Miles Ago and Years Away," and "Peg Leg,"

Hotel Masticadores: "Tomorrow" and "When You Want to Stay but Have to Go,"

Amethyst Review: "Cristo Redentor" and "Five-Year-Old Eyes" and "Feeling Good,"

formidable woman sanctuary: "Crazy for My River, Crazy for Her"

Gasconade Review: "Driving Off, Minor"

Chewers Masticadores: "That's All" and "All Blues,"

Literary Revelations: "New Heights, with Coltrane," "Driving Back to a Love Supreme"

In addition, thanks go to Osage Arts Community for their support of poetry in the region.

Table of Contents:

Drop all your work, leave it behind
Forget all your problems and get in my car
And take a drive with me

-The Kinks, Drivin

This collection is dedicated to Justin, Ryan, Alyssa, and Bonnie, each one my destination.

On my trips from Missouri to Cleveland and Buffalo, I would write while driving – dictate to my phone – inspired by sights along the way and thoughts about my trip and destination. Often, those sights and thoughts might also be inspired by music I was playing at the time, but I might also later consider music that complemented my words. *Random Riffs* were born. I've also written some inspired by hiking and kayaking, but driving is the main theme, including many other destinations over the past couple of years. The *song*, *instrumental*, or *album* that inspired each poem appears as a subtitle.

Truckin'

Truckin' / The Grateful Dead

The Dead play
as wheels turn,
carry us north,
east of where we were, south
of where we want to be,
and I glance at our speed,
prompted by the sight
of a cop on a bridge,
radar gun in hand,
who glances up at a jet
contrail of conspiratorial origin
left by a pilot radioing
the location of an object
of unidentified nature
on a long strange trip of its own,
a smuggler's run
from a secret Chinese moon
base producing aerospace
tech products, where terraforming
efforts advance at an accelerated rate,
rubber trees nearly ready to roll out
the next set of tires for future daydreams
to Buffalo and home again.

Leaving Kansas with Jimi

Electric Lady Land (album) / Jimi Hendrix

No crosstown traffic here.
We're talking cross country.
Yellow fields on the left,
yellow fields on the right,
a foot tall and waiting for a chance
to be in your next wheat beer.

Driving into the morning sun,
you thought you were leaving
gray skies behind, but when you see
that straight and narrow ribbon of a road
disappear at the crest of a hill
four miles ahead framed by black sky
punctuated by jagged bolts of lightning
you know there won't be any magic
carpet in this electric lady land.

The rain starts slow and lazy at first
as Jimi's guitar dances with a sax,
but five minutes later, you drive into
a rainy day that may as well be
a long hot summer night and wish
it was all a daydream. Rain lashes
your windshield, and thirty feet
is the farthest you can see,
so you slow to thirty and hope
you're still pointed straight ahead.

But then, as if tonight's full moon
was turning the tides gently away,
you burst through the last of it
to find a patch of blue sky
as you head out of Kansas,
thankful to have that behind you
and looking forward to that beer.

Drivin' with Primus

Southbound Pachyderm / Primus

Well, that was not a planned stop.

Take powdery snow on a slick, wet road.
Throw in an RV rollin' over
in front of me, blockin' the interstate.
Now, if that ain't rude!
That's a city boy for you,
drivin' like that in the winter.

Sit there in the cold and dark, waitin' for 'em
to haul that crushed rollin' cabin outta there.
When traffic starts crawlin' again,
slippin' and slidin' along, it might as well be
a southbound pachyderm.
That's when I know it's time to get off
at Terre Haute and park my ass in a hotel.

But now it's mornin',
and it's back on the road, again,
Les talkin' to me with his bass,
remindin' me I'll do anything to get there
so my baby can lie down by my side.
I think I'll just let that fat bass drive me home.

Drivin' Under the Influence

One Bourbon, One Scotch, One Beer / George Thorogood

I have no love lost
for lake effect snow
or the blinding whiteouts
of Western New York weather.
I just take it as it comes.

And when it comes down
like this, slow and steady,
it's like George strumming
that backbeat. But up ahead
there's a wall of white,
and I can feel his raw notes,
all the while thinkin' about
my baby scratchin' my back
when I get back home.

I know this snow won't last
forever, and when I get back
to Missouri I'll be askin' where
winter went. When bare trees
are the only accent
on a brown landscape
that makes me miss lake effect
snow, the one consolation is my baby
waiting to pour me a drink.

Forget the bourbon.
But one scotch and one beer?
Hell, yeah.

Driving with Brubeck

Take Five / The Dave Brubeck Quartet

Concrete seams click beneath
the rapid turn of wheels

trying to impress the need
for arrival, as a sax greets an expanse of blue

waving on a horizon breaking free
of its cloudy blanket, revealing

more blue as grapevines,
in row after orderly row, march

up a snow covered slope,
drummer keeping the beat.

Gulls wander in from the lake,
and hilltop turbines can't keep up.

Five takes, and no photo worthy of saving.
This ain't no St. Louis, but the sky is still blue.

New Heights, with Coltrane

Ascension (album) / John Coltrane

that voice, among a frenzied pulse
of voices in Ascension,
their window brief

each branch outreaching the next,
never reaching the eagle as it banks,
passing overhead

as the tires drone, alive
with a pulse that thrives,
even as it succumbs

to a pulse that rises
even as it falls,
no missed beat

as the eagle continues
to rise, never faltering,
even as the sun sets

Riding with Monk

1957 Riverside Recordings (album) / Thelonious Monk

Epistrophy, apostrophe,
brush these blues off of me.
Lift me off this loneliest of roads,
beyond these bare trees.

Even in their beauty,
these bones of winter
hold no answers,
only questions.

On this road of introspection,
you tease me with those keys.
I don't blame you, but
I've had all the blues I can abide.

I'm not in the mood.
Give it to me straight.
I'm tired of chasing dreams.
Lend me yours.

It doesn't have to be easy,
but these streets would look
a whole lot better with
blue skies and just a little green.

A Love Supreme

A Love Supreme / John Coltrane

there is one
single
sole
primary
absolute reason
I live so far from
those I love
the place I call home
visited less often
than desire would have
Acknowledgment long held

the highway passing
before
behind me

my thoughts here
back
ahead
keys that build
to a frenetic pace
as Coltrane offers
Resolution

until the drums roll
with the road
duel with those keys
draw his saxophone back

in Pursuance of
a Psalm, a calm
to remind me
balance can be found
in *A Love Supreme*

Driving Off, Minor

Off Minor / Thelonious Monk with John Coltrane

Monk spars with Coltrane,
weaves around and through him.
They roll along amid lightning strikes
that illuminate the dark sky.
Mist rises from the road's surface
in this dusk of midafternoon on a gray April day
with light rain that is reflected, multiplied,
rises to join that mist from the tires of passing cars
before joining the sheen of the road's surface
in my headlights. The sky before me opens
to reveal a road not so dark and hazards
behind me. Monk's piano never off, minor
discordance trails off to better roads.

Roaming Wyoming with Mingus

Better Git It in Your Soul / Charles Mingus

Ah um, yeah,
that's right.
You can wind your way
through these hills.

Feel that beat? That rhythm?
That's you, just rolling along.
Clear roads. Clear sailing.

But you saw those gates
on the interstate.
And that haze on the mountains?
It may be the last week of March,
but winter lives here,
and you're just a visitor.

That's right, snow.
And by the time you get to Casper,
it'll be waitin' for you.

So feel that sax.
Git it in your soul.
You're here to say goodbye,
and dark skies are fitting.

There will be blue skies
when you come out
on the other side of this,
so roll with the beat.

Frank Morgan at the Wheel

Mood Indigo (album) / Frank Morgan

We may be out of Wyoming,
but that doesn't change a thing.
She's still gone, and the mood
won't be any less indigo.

Nothing but gray skies, and the snow
insists on following. It won't let up,
let you forget, and insists on bringing
blues deeper than any Bessie ever knew.

When a moment alone seemed like a lifetime
the blues took hold of her. They're not
going anywhere, even if she's gone.
Not with two left to carry them.

Even the blue that tries to break through
the clouds seems to say you can't escape,
and Frank's sax sitting in for Duke's piano
seems to say the same.

Is it the separation of miles and years
that brings on a sentimental mood?
If only this could be resolved
by something as simple as a lullaby.

Driving with Miles

So What / Miles Davis

Rain falls, steady, and I say so what.
Wipers try in vain to keep the beat,
but this combo is too tight.
The bass just layin' it down,
horn and sax sparring.

There's a fog rolling through the hills,
tellin' the rain
hold the ice, this is just too cool.

Bare branches, with pines the only green
in a landscape of white on brown.

Wait!
A lone birch like a ghost that knows.
As blue as this feels,
there will be no blue sky.

And that so what refrain slips in
and out.

Narrow roads now,
winding through wet grass
lined with granite and marble.
A memorial among memorials,
some barely legible.
Everything here is blue,

except the pines, white now with big, heavy flakes.
Country roads skirt the mountains,
Snow, now powder, hangs in the air
like a fog. Roads slicker than the music.

Hands tense on the wheel.
Piano eases through me, slowly
levels out, brings me back to the lake,
out there somewhere,
blue asleep within the white.

Riding in Comfort to Kingston

Pork Soda / Primus

That RV hanging off the back of a wrecker
is weaving back and forth on the highway
to Kingston with the back wall blown right off.

I'm riding with John Dorsey, and we both know
there's got to be one helluva story behind it.
Looking inside, it's almost all gone.

There's not even a kitchen sink in there,
but stretched across the back of the trailer
is a plush leather couch that looks

a lot more comfortable than the seats
we're sitting in. Is it burgundy?
Hell, I don't know, but I can almost see

Les Claypool putting his feet up
swilling down a can of pork soda
and thinking this'll never fit in the garage.

Meanwhile, John's wishing they would
head to Barb's Books. A couch like that
would be perfect for poetry readings.

Rainy Day

Rainy Day, Dream Away / Jimi Hendrix

Sax and organ, back and forth,
dance with Jimi's guitar,
the drums laying it down
between, beneath them.
All of it laid back and smooth,
a nice counter to the rain
pelting the windshield
as we head past Boonville, I-70
a sheen with fractured taillights
on one side and headlights sparkling
on the other. My grip on the wheel
loosens as the music soothes me,
a light touch that's needed
after a sleepless night waiting
for this trip to begin, be over.
Then Jimi tells me to dream away
on this rainy day, groove on this gift
of nature as the sun takes a holiday.
I'm reminded that we've been hammered
by a heatwave and drought, and this rain
is what we need. Heading westward,
holding steady at seventy, I ride out the rain
as Jimi's guitar really comes alive,
ripping through those sheets of rain
until it's just a mist clinging to the trees.
And he's right, it did drain my worries away.

I Can't Drive 55

I Can't Drive 55 / Sammy Hagar

LA's not even in the picture,
because I'm headed east
out of Wyoming through
gold-topped cornfields.
When I come up on bales
upon bales of hay, lined up
and envious of the traffic
flying by while they sit
round and ready to roll,
Sammy says to pick up the pace,
ignore that 55mph speed limit
on my U-Haul trailer's fender.
So I put my foot on the gas
and follow the Nebraska signs
that say 75 is the way to go.

Still, with no cops in sight, cars
pass me by, leave me in their dust.
Yeah, they'll make it to Lincoln,
dead or alive.

Radar Love

Radar Love / Golden Earring

Occasional headlights
the only break in the darkness,
I count white lines
that flash before me, each one
closer to my destination.

This road knows me well.
Every curve wraps itself
around me. The rumble strip
knows my name, warns
of the siren of sleep that beckons

with a trance that lures me
to be anywhere but where I am.
Mile markers pass beside me,
the road beneath me. I remain
a stationary element in the night,

until I'm lifted by a guitar intro
that leads into a steady drum beat.
The wheel goes light in my hands,
and I hear my baby's voice,
her longing calling me home.

That drumbeat carries me along,
and there's a glow on the horizon
as the sun slowly rises,
but I won't let it blind me to my goal.

I need her as much as she needs me.

I keep a steady pace, feel the comfort
she sends my way. There's no way
I'll let the road keep me hypnotized.
She's my light in the sky, and I know
her radar love will bring me home safe.

Miles Ago and Years Away

I Can See for Miles / The Who

thirteen and fourteen during those summers
sleeping bag and a rolled-up shirt
for bedding, we slept in the backyard
John's, Mike's, mine, in rotation
every weekend under the stars
not that we slept all that much

too much to do and never enough darkness
especially if a yard light came on
as we hopped into a neighbor's pool,
skinny dipping of course, the neighbor
yelling as we made our exit
bare-assed and clutching our clothes

on to the next adventure, yard to yard
I'm sure those people finally sold their house
but it probably didn't help
when they woke every Saturday morning
to find their For Sale sign
sitting on their neighbor's front lawn

and that garage with a covered side patio
sure came in handy, not that we needed a garage
but the picnic table was a nice spot to sit
and have a beer from the tap in the wall
I wonder if that guy ever figured out
why his keg of Schmidt's emptied so fast

or that Sunday morning, when I walked to John's house
I Can See for Miles playing on my transistor
parents asleep, as he loaded the Courier Express
into his mom's '62 Cadillac and told me to hop in
he drove, I ran the papers, and the Caddy was back
in the garage before his dad was any the wiser

skinny dipping and swapping For Sale signs
are decades behind me, and good luck
finding a bottle of Schmidt's – give me craft beer
any time, preferably a stout – but every time
I read the Sunday funnies I can see for miles
as I think of that joy ride back in '67

You Can Drive My Car

Drive My Car / The Beatles

Your prospects were good,
but now there's a cloud
over your head
and your car won't start,
breaks your heart
in the breakdown lane
as you wait for a tow
in the middle of the night.

With nothing to do in between
and no juice to raise the top,
you sit back to watch
a meteor shower and count
those shooting stars until,
beep-beep, yeah,
the tow truck is here.

It'll take a lot more than peanuts
to get this fixed. All you can do
is hope for better times,
'cause you've got no car
and it's breaking your heart.

After the Rain

After the Rain / John Coltrane

Piano opens with a crash,
trails off to reveal percussion
and bass lying just below it.

A friend is gone
and the moment is empty.

Revealing the sax,
like a lament holding
the hope that left with him.

An icy shore scoured by bitter
winter winds holds no memories.

Piano comes forward,
as if holding light after a storm,
and the sax takes a lighter tone.

Come the spring rain, voice
and thoughts once lost will return.

The cymbal's last sound is a gentle
parting as sax and piano trail off,
as if Coltrane knows it will be alright.

Explorations

Explorations (album) / Bill Evans Trio

Driving,
once again at night,
but it's not the darkness
that brings inspiration

as I leave Kansas City.
I consider a day
spent with poets,
a day of exploration,
one that confirms
there is life in poetry.

Never staying in one place,
Bill Evans' piano
underscores that, with
Scott LaFaro's baseline
the pulse that carries my thoughts
forward, quickening at times,
a heartbeat that responds
to words that still echo
in my mind.

Writers,
from readings to open mic,
shared methods,
perspectives,
in a tempo that varied
from moment to moment.

Paul Motian's percussive
staccato is a reminder of
those different directions
that felt as natural as
a brush on cymbals.

How does a trio
encapsulate
an experience in this way?
I wish I knew.

C Jam Blues

C Jam Blues / Charles Mingus

Hoppin', boppin'.
Strollin' along.
Who is this cat?

Is he the bass,
layin' down that smooth beat?
The piano, weavin'
highlights in and out?

No, man.
He's the sax,
with places to go
and people to see.
He ain't sittin' still
for nothin'.

But what's he thinkin',
his route takin' him
where he don't belong,
headin' north where
I-70's goin' east, more than 70?

Then there's that hoppin',
that armadillo startled jump,
straight up as a pickup
passes right over him.

So there he lies
feet up, his shell
flattened as a semi
crosses his path.

And this jam ends,
a long fade out
of a wail,
as if Mingus knows.

Ascenseur pour l'echafaud

Ascenseur pour l'echafaud (album) / Miles Davis

Bad news seems to come at every turn,
friends facing dark skies.
On my way to see my own doctor,
I wonder if it's my turn. North on 63
out of Jeff City, climbing hill after hill
with Columbia always beyond the horizon,
I leave gray skies behind to drive
into some of the darkest I've seen.
This may not be an elevator,
but each time I crest a hill I wonder
if I'll find gallows at the top,
faceless friends lined up
to the plaintive wail of Miles' trumpet
as they wait for their turn in this film noir,
wait for me to join them, my heartbeat
the bass that lies under every track.
But then that trumpet almost sings.
And even when that horn is muted
I know that we each have our own highway,
and not every road leads to the gallows.

Cristo Redentor

Cristo Redentor / Donald Byrd

A haunting chorale
laced with sonorous chords
leads me through winding hills
to deliver me
into the narrow valley
that holds Westphalia,
where a church spire high on a hill
rises from surrounding trees to be seen
by all who pass on the highway
below, both wayward and devout.

As I leave that steeple behind,
Donald Byrd's trumpet,
slow, and almost sultry, moves in,
dances with those voices,
and Duke Pearson's piano teases,
seems to offer a revelation.

Rich Fountain lies just down the road,
waits to follow suit, its church
again totally obscured above me,
save the lines of its spire
rising above the trees.

When the road from there
opens to a wide valley,
I almost expect to see
Sugarloaf Mountain on the horizon

with the arms of Christ the Redeemer
opened wide, expecting me to come home.

Once baptized,
that boat long since capsized,
I still know all the rituals,
mouth the words at weddings
and funerals, though I know
they'll never be uttered at mine.

As if knowing that ship has sailed,
trumpet, piano, and chorale
fade into the distance
as I head down the road to Belle.

Light Years

2000 Light Years from Home / The Rolling Stones

East on I-70, halfway
between Missouri and Buffalo.
Am I just a rolling stone
moving back and forth
between two places
that mean so much to me?

Sailing past Dayton,
where jets in formation
grace the pylons
of the interchange
as if heading into space
while alien starships
at Wright-Patterson cast a spell
that pushes and pulls me
in both directions. Family
ahead and behind me
as waves of energy
echo in the music. Is it them
or is it me that's too many
light years from home?
How can I be satisfied,
yet so lonely,
when both places are home?

Tomorrow

Tomorrow Never Knows / The Beatles

a sitar drones, thoughts
drum through my mind,
ease into acceptance

west on I-70 to KC
then north & west
North Platte, eventually
– tomorrow, Casper

gray trip
on a gray day
beads on the windshield
can't obscure the loss
waiting at the other end

semis the whole way
shedding worn treads
my road unclear
drums and vocals urge me
to lay down all thoughts
but mine stay in the present

still, the words remind me
to know is to believe
that love is all

this grayscape takes on
the colors of my dreams

I may mourn the dead
but I will celebrate the living
nothing expendable
everyone essential

always forward
holding close
those important to me
every day is a new beginning
tomorrow never knows

When You Want to Stay but Have to Go

GO! (album) / Dexter Gordon

Where are you
when the lights go out
and all you can see on I-70
are red lights and headlights?

With Kansas behind us,
are the memories you shared
with family you never see
often enough still in your thoughts,
or did they start to fade
once we left Lawrence?

It may not be 3:00 in the morning,
but we're staring at midnight.
With Dexter's sax and Sonny's piano,
staying awake will be no problem,
so you have a couple of hours
to get this straight in your head.

Leaving was hard to do,
with so much more to know, but
we're halfway home now, with nothing
to stop us from getting there.

Let me watch for headlights
and taillights while you look back
on the memories you shared
and the stories you learned.

Peg Leg

Peg Leg / Ron Carter

With Lincoln in the rearview
and Casper well north of us,
the monotony of heading straight
west across the Nebraska plains
lets my mind stray further
down the road to concerns
about our destination,
an empty house in windswept
Wyoming with no life left to it,
or just enough to cast a pall
over these blue skies.

As we approach North Platte,
Peg Leg starts coming
over the speakers with guitar
and piano almost as one voice
coaxing the drums.
And they don't stop
when Ron Carter comes in
with his piccolo bass, because
now all of them are dancing
and that bass is singing.

Our hotel is two miles straight off
the interstate, but when the piano
takes the lead I make a hard right
as soon as we exit.

It's like this combo knows
that Peg Leg Brewing is right
down the road, a place with great beer
and the same positive vibe.
Where the brewer turns
a handicap into an asset,
with the prosthetics he's worn
through life, shoes and all,
hanging from the ceiling.

I let that piano play out
and soak in more of the bass
as it dances its way to the end
before we walk into the pub.
Just being there, timed perfectly
with music that's full of life,
tells me that things aren't all bad.
We'll head out in the morning,
and I'll make sure that Peg Leg
is playing when we pull into Casper.

All Blues

All Blues / Miles Davis

As I leave my doctor's office
and head south out of Columbia,
I hear a backbeat
joined by light piano and sax,
a surge that could be my heart
responding to the news.

The sky can't decide
if it wants to be pale azure
or white clouds threaded with gray
as I pass December-bare trees
and brown-tinged cedars
that offer no relief.

That beat beneath him, Miles
moves in on trumpet, forlorn,
as I consider the thought of
more labs, more medication,
stress taking its toll.

And still that heartbeat,
as trumpet gives way to sax,
Adderley and Coltrane,
trading notes high and low,
pulling me out of
and back into the blues.

The piano moves up
from the back, almost struggling
to bring some light into the story,
but at this point it's all blues.

The trumpet returns,
just as forlorn, as if telling me
to do something about this,
then fades with that percussive beat
that could be my heart.

Driving Back to a Love Supreme

A Love Supreme (album) / John Coltrane

Layer upon layer of clouds holding
a snow that never materialized
deliver a gray light,
but there's joyful anticipation at the start
of this long drive home like a pulse
of contentment. A love supreme.

Piano pulls me forward with resolve
when Coltrane comes in,
pursuing that love,
as drums urge me onward.

Like a psalm rolling through me,
clouds give way to blue sky,
the hint of home drawing me closer
on this long cold drive.

Roll the Bones

Roll the Bones / Rush

Back in New York
on River Road,
Niagara River beside me.
Every time I drive this stretch
I get a rush, thinking about
that day, 45 years ago.

Accelerating from 45
I approached the light,
where the speed limit changed
to 55, when a car pulled out
and stopped, my path blocked.
Random interaction
leads to action, reaction.

Even at 73 feet per second,
I didn't need math to tell me
I had two seconds to react.
No time to ask why me,
I swerved hard left then right,
back into my lane.

My front wheel danced
in slow-mo at 50 mph,
and my bike took forever
to slide to its side.
I hit the pavement in time
with the handlebars.

Head first, headlight first,
my wheels still spinning,
and the highway passing
below me, going nowhere.

Helmet destroyed and road rash
but no broken bones
after one helluva rush,
I drove that bike home
the next day. Bought a bigger one
the next year and rolled on.
Twelve years later, this time
behind the wheel, Geddy Lee
came on the radio and told me
it happened because it happened.
Roll the bones.

Five-Year-Old Eyes

Requiem (complete) / Wolfgang Mozart

cue Mozart's Requiem Aeternam

One of my trips headed home
from New York's southern tier
to Erie, then on to Cleveland.
From a funeral. Both times.

segue to Dies Irae

The second one, in a blizzard
that had me hoping I'd live
to see Lake Erie on the horizon,
hit too close to home.

transition... Lux Aeterna

But this was the first one,
my first time on those country
back-roads in nearly sixty years.
Driving through Great Valley,
I had to pull on to the shoulder.
I'd been there before.

now Hostias

With five-year-old eyes, I knew
it was the place. I could see it.
An old wood-frame house, just

off the road, hugging the creek bank
behind it like it wanted to fall in
as my little eyes peered over the window
ledge into the water below after
sleeping on the floor among family
I'd never meet again, that part
of my father's life left behind.

and Lacrimosa

Except, it wasn't there. All
that remained was a memory
that woke on that country road
in a mind that welcomed
any reminder of those times.

fade to closing of
Vesperae Solemnos de Confessore

No Place to Go

No Place to Go / Fleetwood Mac (Peter Green)

No traffic here.
Slow easy steps that ride
the beat of the music,
the harmonica bleeding through
like a sob, and Peter Green asking
how much longer can this go on?

I walk the trail, a conservation area,
because that's what it's come to.
You want to see a two-hundred-year-old oak
or a hickory or walnut even taller?
It's getting so you're lucky to see them
in the wild. We set them apart
to protect them from us.

And that harp moves to the front
as the beat continues, as if nature
is wailing at its abuse. And Green asks
again, how much longer can this go on.

I round a bend, and the paved section
transitions to wood chips that cushion
my feet, but not before I step over
a steaming pile of dog crap
in the center of the path, a fitting partner
for the candy wrapper I passed earlier.

The same path that's posted.
No dogs allowed.
But that's the respect we give
to what we're trying to protect.

I walk beneath the trees, my steps heavy
with the beat, as the harmonica wails on,
until, as if giving up, it fades out,
leaving me to wonder. When, at last,
these trees are old and fallen down,
where will we go?

Bridge of Sighs

Bridge of Sighs / Robin Trower

A thousand-mile drive to get here
one last time, the last two on gravel.
Another fifty yards up the drive.

A chime weaves through a lone guitar
as Robin Trower plays a forlorn tune.
We walk past sage and weeds that tumble

in the unending wind. Into the house,
emptied, cleaned of any signs of life,
yet I hear a voice that's speaks out.

No sun will shine, no moonshine
to cleanse this child.

Here by choice, remote, but connected
to the land she loved. Connections
to her family were more tenuous.

A life spent in search of satisfaction,
always over a horizon that betrayed her
with one more of life's cruel tricks.

She was found in the dead of winter,
collapsed after trudging through drifts
to get inside. And the voice continues.

The wind blows cold
on the soul of this poor child.

The guitar continues, backed by
a drum with a slow, deliberate beat,
that chime weaving in and out, haunting.

Out the door and into that Wyoming wind,
we start the long drive home, her home
receding in the rearview mirror.

Never one to leave that part of her
behind, she may be gone, but
she'll always be there.

Cold and unforgiving,
this unending bridge of sighs.

Ad Lib Blues

Ad Lib Blues / Lester Young

Over 900 miles on the road
Time a precious commodity
Interstates the price
Tedium and tolls

South of Canandaigua,
Thruway behind us,
contentment on country roads
between forested hills

Ski slopes to the right
wait for snow
Our destination opposite,
at the end of a winding road

Lester Young on sax
sounds far from blue
layered with Oscar Peterson,
coaxing the piano to the front

We walk into a house
filled with voices,
family gathered,
conversations in layers

Ad libs
Non sequiturs
Laughter
The joy of being together

A guitar is the sunlight
pouring into the wall of windows
on this summer weekend, the delight
echoed in the voices of grandchildren

Sax and piano dance through
our days together, the only blues
coming as they wind down
and we make our separate ways home

Crazy for My River, Crazy for Her

Somewhere Down the Crazy River / Robbie Robertson

Jonesing for those two
great lakes, Erie and Ontario,
with the lifeblood that flows
between them, I quench my thirst
at the mouth of the Niagara,
let lakeshore waves wash
over my feet as water runs
through my hands to reveal
beach glass bluer than those waves.

Now south, along the river
to walk beside its shore,
watch the wind bend cattails
over more blue water and raise
kites high overhead. The rhythm
of bass and drums leaves me
wanting to be nowhere else.
No levee here, but I can hear
Robbie Robertson, a lazy beat
behind him. This river may not
fog my mind, but it does stir my soul,
waves of emotion washing over me.

Further south to the waterfront,
Buffalo skyline behind me
and more blue water before me,
as I watch monarchs make
a brief stop on Lake Erie's shore
before heading further south,

my own path taking me past Erie
and away from all that blue water.

My destination is nowhere near
the Big Easy, yet it's far enough
south to wrap me at times
with its smothering heat.
She knows I can't say the wind
pushed me this way, when
my need to be with her pulled me.

I'll always return to her,
my clear destination, never
a wish to abandon her, even
as my imagination takes me
back to that blue water,
where time seems to stand still.
Now, you might think I'm crazy,
but I'm crazy for both of them
They leave me spellbound.

Feeling Good

Feeling Good / Nina Simone

The sky never alone, even on a cloudless day,
heron, swallows, and cormorants
pass around me. The pace of my paddle
is more in time with the slow rhythm of
the heron than the frantic flight of
the swallows, but as Nina Simone
reminds me, my heart is with them,
and with the few leaves that drift on by
in the early morning summer sun,
still low in the sky and glinting off
the ripples of my wake.

Each season has its rewards,
from blossoms on the trees in spring
to the dragonfly resting on the bow of
my kayak, to the colors of autumn,
to the sheen of ice clinging to
the river shore in late winter,
each season offering the peace of
a new dawn, each new day
a reason to feel good
about what life has to offer.

My strokes are slow and sure with a horn
that plays like a slow march, as if to keep
Nina grounded, her joy likely to carry her
away to the stars. Strings and piano
move in to reflect that joy, with the horn

stepping in again, underlying her words
as if to give weight to such a peaceful feeling.
As her voice trails off, I continue
to paddle along the shore, feeling good.

Nothing but Time

Time / Pink Floyd

The clock ticks,
as it always does.
An alarm rings,
or does it?
There hasn't been one
dull day, as alarms
have been going off
for the past week.

Doctors think they know,
but do they?
So they send me on a road trip,
my gurney boosted
into the back of the bus.
It's hard to believe
I now call this my hometown,
but I leave it behind
as we head into the night.

Looking back at headlights,
taillights, I wonder
if I've frittered, wasted
the years that are behind me.
But no one was going to show me,
so I made my own way.
I've lived each moment,
and nothing can take that from me.

I once was young,
and life was always long.
Until it wasn't.
But that doesn't mean
that each day doesn't have
its own starting gun.

Waters and Gilmour may not
expect me to catch up with the sun,
but I know it's waiting,
offering me a new day. I'll always be
older, and I may be short of breath,
but death will have to wait.
I'll take every minute, every
scribbled line that comes my way,
save them, learn from them
until I'm finally home.

It's just past midnight as we pull up
to the hospital in St. Louis.
I know my past is always
a part of me, but this is a new day
and I'm ready to make more memories.

Road to Recovery

Blue Rondo à La Turk / The Dave Brubeck Quartet

Piano starts out fast,
joined by the sax, almost
racing, both trying to be
first one out the door.

You're right there with them.
After nearly three weeks,
it's time to get as far from
that hospital as possible.

Piano and sax take turns
urging you on. It's 126 miles.
Let's get a move on.
Home is waiting for you.

Pack your bags. Make that one.
It may be 18 days, but the clothes
you started with will get you home.
Load it into the truck.

The alto sax seems to be
the first to understand as
Paul Edmonds slows the pace,
Brubeck's piano still nudging him.

It's a slow climb into the truck
as you pause to catch your breath.
Underlying bass and drums finally
pull the piano in line with the sax.

You're a passenger today,
first time in a very long time.
Relax. Seat back, feet up.
Let that combo seep into you

as it seems to stroll along
right next to, into, you.
Let it set the pace for you
on that long ride home.

That's All

That's All / Lee Morgan

Driving home from St. Louis,
election news on my mind,
when Lee Morgan comes in on trumpet,
soft, almost forlorn, as if he's heard
the bad news. Dark days are coming,
and it's not just politics.
It's what the politics brings,
and this election has cast a shadow
over our country. Near dusk,
a giant orange orb casts an eerie glow
as it lurks beyond the horizon.
Hank Jones' piano seems to lie
beneath the trumpet, softening the blow
a bit, until the trumpet comes to life,
as if to draw my thoughts
down the road and across the years,
when we can try to recover from
the damage of these next four years.
Morgan's trumpet closes with
those forlorn tones, and all we can do
is hope we survive to tell him *that's all.*

Ken Gierke is a transplanted Western New Yorker, moving in retirement to mid-Missouri in 2012. He is a Pushcart Prize nominee, and his poetry has appeared in numerous anthologies. His poetry collections, *Glass Awash* in 2022 and *Heron Spirit* in 2024, were published by Spartan Press.

This project was made possible, in part, by generous support from the Osage Arts Community.

Osage Arts Community provides temporary time, space and support for the creation of new artistic works in a retreat format, serving creative people of all kinds — visual artists, composers, poets, fiction and nonfiction writers. Located on a 152-acre farm in an isolated rural mountainside setting in Central Missouri and bordered by ¾ of a mile of the Gasconade River, OAC provides residencies to those working alone, as well as welcoming collaborative teams, offering living space and workspace in a country environment to emerging and mid-career artists. For more information, visit us at www.osageac.org

Osage Arts Community